MISCHIEF

MISCHIEF

John Terpstra

GASPEREAU PRESS ¶ PRINTERS & PUBLISHERS 2017

To my co-mischief-makers

Poetry Burns

A Hamilton man is facing charges
after setting fire to a mattress
in his MacNab Street North apartment.

Police say the man
who lives on the fourth floor of the fourteen-storey building

covered his bed with pages of poetry
before setting it ablaze
          around 7 p.m. Tuesday.

He then ran into the hallway and pulled the fire alarm.

The fire was confined to one apartment
and quickly put out by firefighters.

Tenants were not evacuated.
Detectives are continuing to probe the incident.

A 37-year-old man is charged with arson
and mischief
                    endangering life.

MISCHIEF

All My Glory

The trees have stopped talking to me.
The tulip tree with its big yellow leaves
just stands there, dropping them
in silence.

Ditto the apple. Even the tree of heaven.

Our backyard conversations in the past were brief
but always intense. Truly,

it was more about presence, attendance,
and spending the time,
than words.

Walking through their company in the valley,
my path was another branch,
the creek their sap.

Our sap.
It was magical.
I would ask for those days back again,

but why?
The trees have always known me better
than I know myself.

I stand
in all my glory,
what glory I have,
stilled and wondering,

losing my grip on one leaf after the other,

and feel not
at all
like talking.

North of Sixty

I greet you from the other side of the river.
I wave my hand.
What river? you ask. *I don't see a river.*
Neither did I, is my reply.
Not until I stepped into it.

I like to think that I still own property
on your side of the river,
and will come visit, stay a few days.
But who am I fooling?
It's time to sell.

I can tell you that the landscape here
is different, but the same. Mostly trees.
My sense is
mountains ahead. Something about the air.

Here's a surprise: we've taken up dancing, most nights,
when no one is watching.
We're still a little awkward and shy
with each other, to be honest,
and getting used to looking into each other's eyes,
which is one of the rules. But it's like
early days. Imagine:
like early days.

On this side of the river my sense is the days
nest rather than follow, one then the next.
That may explain it.

One of us takes the sleeping bag
and stretches out full-length under the stars
while the other collects round stones on the beach
and five, six, seven high,
stacks them.

We've never been in it for the money:
I don't have to tell you that.
Now all our chickens are coming home,
and surprise surprise, it's an Easter egg hunt out here.
It's like with all those kids we saw in the park last spring.
Imagine.

Night Bus

In the middle of the night, having risen
for the usual reason, now listening
to the trailing drips of water's rush
through plumbing, you are alone again
in the dark.
                    A single street light illumines
the patch of concrete where you stand
waiting for the bus, hoping
it will come, that you haven't missed it,
the last bus, destination not
                                        Downtown
or *Chicago*, but
                    Sleep.

                                You picture it
emerge through the gloom, grow large,
and stop at the curb with a nasal wheeze.
The narrow doors split and fold aside,
and you step up. You have never
lost the pleasure of coin's clatter
in the glass-sided box,
or the driver's sleight-of-hand
that drops the box bottom,
                                        vanishing your fare.
The sound rattles the air
                                    as you drift back
in search of a seat, though none is taken.
Behind you, the driver has risen to his feet,
and reaches to wind the chrome hand-crank
that scrolls through the place-names of your mind,

while humming. You turn to sit and face
the wide-screen windshield, and are falling
deeply
          into its CinemaScope narrative

when the bell dings
                    to indicate your stop
and your hand reaches reflexively
for the cord,
              to un-pull, if it can,
before the screen goes blank
and the lights come on,
the plug
          on that damned electric alarm.

Neighbour

This year, the above-ground pool
around whose narrow edge he balanced
early each morning
skimming leaves, debris and insects
with his long pole
like a gondolier
remains unopened.
It was meditation
simply to watch him, and,
while he wasn't looking,
a mother raccoon with fine black fingers
showing the way of cleanliness
to her five kits balanced
on the same edge.
All that water, undisturbed
by children,
the late night dip and swim across
with his widow.

A Common Thread

This is for the guy
who walks down the middle of Cannon Street
jingling the coins in his trench coat pocket
smoking a cigarette
talking out loud
and not walking in a straight line
          but not because he has been drinking.

This is for the woman
straight from Act I, Scene i of *Macbeth*
muttering
pushing her overflowing shopping cart
          cauldron
          of stuffed plastic bags
along York Boulevard.

This is for the skinny guy
with the long beard
wearing only a pair of short-shorts
bent over the handlebars of his ten-speed bicycle
keeping up with traffic
          from one end of the city to the other.

There's a story there
          I think, whenever he speeds by,
That's how he *deals with it.*

This is also for the guy
          who couldn't deal with it
who left the halfway house

across from the mall
went in
and stabbed a woman he'd never met before
 who owned the framing shop.

This is for that woman too
 and for her family and friends
 and the people at the mall
 strangers who came to help her
and to hold him

because in public and in private
wounded or wounding
we all suffer
 and suffer each other
and everyone, as the song goes,
 hurts.

*

This is for everyone
 and anyone
who has ever felt themselves
 hanging by a thread.

This is for how
 alone it feels.

This is not for, but against, the voices

the voices
that are no harmonic chorus
to the soundtrack of life
but a mean-spirited, crazy-making cacophony
that doesn't shut up.

This is for what it takes
to lower their volume
to keep their barking and bullying and lying
at bay
their insinuations, delusions, demands

for what it takes
to not listen
not obey.

This is for how normal and balanced
most of the time
most of us
appear.

This is for the walking, the cycling,
the collecting, the jingling of coins in the pocket,
the harmonica playing, the dancing,
the drawing, the painting—
the thousand and more painstaking paintings
in bright colours
that leap out at you
when you open the gallery door.

This is for everyone
who goes past this building
during the course of a day.

This is for the broken
the irreparable
the family that does what it can
that can only watch.

This is for learning what it is like
at the harder edges
of being human.

This is for getting from one end of the day to the other
day after day
somehow.

This is for anyone
and everyone
and their thread

a common thread.

This is a prayer
it be well-braided.

Near-Annunciation at Carroll's Point

First try, the bird dropped
                                        from the sky,
belly-flopping the surface
that separates our two worlds,
and came up empty.
                                He rose again
and wung away
in easy, languorous strokes,
as if it was all part of the plan.

Hunger returned him.
But whose?

What surprises us now, despite
our dragnet of the seven seas,

is that our lady
was not
         a first or only choice.

I am but a carpenter
sitting on a bench, beside water,
yet have observed
more than one
                    slim silver beauty

who had but a single
                              premonitory moment
to ponder who or what
        that brilliance meant

which filled the sky
before being plucked from their lives.

The dying-to-self
our mothers did so well
a little something
they picked up on the fly.

Plight

Sorrow
is backed up at your border.

It is another day in the life of the world
on its head.

Sorrow and need
are lined up
and leaning against the line
you have drawn around yourself.

Sorrow and need,
fear and desperation,
broken walls, broken water mains, broken limbs,

and people,
far too many people,
are massed at your gate.

Let them in.
Feel overwhelmed,
but let them in.

Feed them,
clothe and house,
care for and school their children.
Find work for their hands.

Sing them your songs.

Learn theirs.

Yes. Ask
to learn their lost songs of home.

Crossings

Her device held with two hands before a slightly bowed head,
a young woman floats across the intersection
like a nun with her breviary, her Book of Hours,
and is so deeply absorbed in its consolations and instruction
that her crossing, in the imaginations of the drivers
who are waiting to turn, takes hours.

The only times we humans are allowed to hold up traffic
is at crossings like these,
            or in transit to the grave,
although in the larger cities this is no longer universally true,
and I wonder, do cars on both sides of the road
still come to a complete stop in Chatham, Ontario,
            a rural city of forty-four thousand,
as they did several years ago, on the day
we slowly crossed his hometown
in my best friend's father's procession?

Every day, thousands of people
climb into their personal craft
to begin a crossing. I see them now
stepping in as they push their vessels
through the shoreline waves
            of one of the beaches of Toronto,
picking up a paddle as they set off,
paddling not to anything so grand
as their own death or burial
but only to the far side of the day.

Each morning thousands climb

over the edge of the mattress
that has rafted them through the night
and step onto water
that is disguised as carpet or hardwood,
trying not to look down or think too much
about what they are doing, because
it is patently not possible,
anyone can see that,
all you can do is wish for the best
and give a hand if needed
as you would to someone who is crossing the street.

The young woman reaches the curb at last,
and as traffic resumes its flow through
this commercial-industrial-residential intersection
of the North Service Road and nowhere
she floats on
to the shopping mall.

Pray for us, sister. Now
and at that hour. Keep on
praying for us all.

Old Religion

In the park opposite the cemetery
someone's digging precise rectangles
inch by inch deeper
with a spoon.

From the boulevard
you can see the squat pyramid
of loose soil, straddled
by a makeshift sieve
and the sawhorse and plywood table
on which whatever does not
sift through the metal mesh
is laid out in neat rows
awaiting closer inspection,
a gentle brushing-clean
and entry onto the pages of a three-ring binder.

The motionless leaves.
The breathless heat and humidity.
The surge of other heat you feel
while driving past, on the off-chance
that all those grave little things
you ever did, and dropped and forgot,
will be dug up, documented and displayed
on that celestial day
            in all their broken beauty.

Needlecraft

In the church where we go to now
the words of the preacher
begin innocently enough
to thread through the fabric of our lives.
They draw together shapes
not previously recognized,
and connect portions of the narrative
as yet unread, or not yet readable,
a pattern not apparent,
as though written and stitched
by a random hand.

The church where we go to now
is, and is not, the church
of our fathers and mothers.
The old words do not come easily,
here, the songs have faded and frayed,
they have been crushed and ground
by the lives of our forebears,
the weighing-down of history.

The preacher is not innocent.
She is both fearful and full of joy.
She would unburden us,
but the slim silver sliver that she guides
will prick
as it moves through,
and there is blood on the pattern,
the page, on the hand,

as well as healing,
just as there was for our mothers and fathers.

She pulls the thread, taut,
then snaps it between her teeth.
Amen. For now and forever
amen to this bite of a new
dispensation, ancient
and exact
as needlecraft.

The Preacher Refuses Baptism to the Author of L'Étranger

He was in your hands, Reverend.
By your own account
he placed himself
          in your hands, asking
was there anything to prevent
          his dipping in or sprinkling,
having stopped to talk with you
beside the waters of the gospel.

Years later, you stop beside the tree
his car made famous, think
suicide, and almost
second-guess
your refusal of his request,
swallowing your pride
that a man may have died
          for a sin you do not confess.

You tell this story now
to a world that questions
the truth
          or possibility
that fifty years past
a French secular saint
revealed his secret heart
to a visiting preacher of the American Church
          in Paris
          over several summers in the 1950s,
a man whom he also
swore to silence.

In the end you can't resist
saving the famous author
          for your life's dessert,
baptizing your readers
with words
          drizzled over the page
where they crystallize
and lie
          like shattered tempered glass
          in the grass surrounding
                    a shattered car.

AFTER READING HOWARD MUMMA,
ALBERT CAMUS AND THE MINISTER.

Orange and Spices

1.

When Charles Darwin sat down, finally
to write his big book,
he wondered, not
how it would end, but where
on the shelf
it would end up.
Lucky for him, over the eons
librarians
have evolved
to be among the sharpest of the species,
able to connect dots and make great
intuitive leaps
between works of fact
and other acts of imagination.
They'd know where his story slipped-in
best and fittest.

2.

A first-year college student raises the sash
of his second-floor rented room and creeps,
like a cat, onto the shingled roof
of the porch below,
over which the orange moon
hangs, or is hung—
over which, on the open page
of his Modern Art text, a moo cow, a newly married

kissing couple, and a tree
jump, hang, or simply
drift. He is a bungalow boy, raised
on wide streets—and all the while
the world is multi-storied?
His heart leaps. And what is
this fragrance, carried wafting through the leaves?
From which island?

3.

In great faith and firm conviction, the world
behaves,
unfolding open wide and wider,
a flower mouthing miracle of detail
that changes and remains the same
under the observing eye
of Mr. Darwin
who plods through time and sentence,
chart and drawing, wondering
who or what the object is,
jumping
(at times) up and down at the dawn
of all things, in spiced delight,
excitement
over
the moon, the orange moon.

4.

The smartest move I ever made was to marry
a librarian. They have the best, most select
stories. A first-year college student approaches the desk
and asks for a book his professor has assigned:
Orange and Spices.
Someone, the librarian thinks,
has been drifting, dreaming sights and smells
of equatorial seas, while seated in class.
She politely repeats, *Orange and Spices*—
which class is that? Biology, the student replies.
And in the pause between one heartbeat and the next
the librarian leaps
from the jungle where all is one
mass of leaf
and retrieves, picks, as it were, fruit from the shelf:
you mean, she asks, *The Origin of Species?*

5.

On the sixth day, Sir Charles Darwin
closes the book
on everything he saw and experienced
when he was so very young, all those years ago,
the boat, the islands. So serendipitous,
that he travelled at all. Creation is good. Fruit is good.
He peels another, and chooses a round, pony hair
No.4 brush, dips it in the glass, and begins
his next watercolour creation.

The Tin Box

I used to wonder what was in the small metal box
that I carted with me everywhere, I've been told,
when I was three years old, and which appears
in the photographs my mother assembled
into the album she stitched and sewed by hand,
and sent to my father's father, after whom I was named,
back home in Holland, *voor Pake's verjaardag*.

Pake and Beppe would have loved this birthday gift.
What's not to love about the eldest son of their eldest son
leaping from bed with a big smile on his mug,
or rolling on the carpet with his two older sisters?
What's not to love but his absence?

For I am the hole in my grandparents' lives—this too
I have been told. I am their abandonment.
I am also the lost and desolate, immigrant feeling
my mother brought to the project—this
I picked up on my own. And how close
it all seems. Elder now to them all,
I too love the young boy in those photos.
What's not to love

about the deer-caught-in-the-headlights look
in one shot, the wanting-to-please, or -perform, in another?
What's not to love but the loss? He sleeps
well and sweetly on the closing page
of this day in his life: on his back, arms flung wide,
and with nothing soft or stuffed to clutch or comfort
as he falls through the branches of the family tree

but a small tin box
that leans against the side wall of the crib,
his soul to keep.

Catechism Class

Saturday mornings in winter, when I was ten,
while others watched cartoons on television,
I caught the Number Two bus, transferred to the Five,
and then walked a few blocks, my mind occupied

with the last-minute memorization
that would see me through catechism class.
Is the heavy artillery of theology still aimed on children?
Undoubtedly. I should have a stronger opinion

as to whether this was good or bad,
and, at one time, I did. The teachers were kind.
On the journey home, anticipating lunch
and my mother's baking, I'd wait for my bus transfer

inside a furniture store, attracted by the warmth
and the deejay from my second-favourite radio station
broadcasting live, songs with titles such as *Da Doo Ron Ron,*
and *It's My Party*. I even won that weekly contrast once.

Contest. I won their contest and received a prize,
and believed what I was told, and deeply internalized it all,
and this has created the tension that has produced,
if I may say, some of my strongest work –

although you shouldn't be surprised if that's not the whole story.

After Catechism Class

On those days
when it was so cold in that northern city
we were told not to run, for fear
the freezing air would crystallize
on our lungs, and we'd die or something,

we walked from the church basement room
where we were asked questions
such as *What is your only comfort*
in life and death?
                        and, *How do you know*
your sin and misery?
                            and answered
from memory, by the book,

                                        we walked
and we ran, ignoring the temperature,
four blocks to the bus stop, and past
a factory bakery churning out thousands
of identical loaves, but not able to hide
the natural processes
which made such vast control
possible,
              processes that ambushed our progress
with warm and fragrant breath
breathed on us
                          from a wall vent
and wafting up
                          simultaneously
through the sidewalk grate.

It was total immersion; baptism
in a brief, other world,
better than this one, gentler, more kind.

Vocation

I can see myself lying on my stomach
on the mattress, beneath a sloped bedroom
ceiling, listening to the radio all summer
because I had nothing else to do.

Because I had nothing else to do but
lie on my bed and listen to the radio, for what
seemed like the entire summer vacation,
I developed a comprehensive knowledge
            of the top-forty radio hit songs.

Much of that three-minute music
was forgettable, although I have not forgotten it.
In between were songs that made the wait worthwhile.
And they all shared in that free articulation of feeling.

The free articulation of feeling. How did they do it?
I thought I was bored and had nothing to do.
Meanwhile, the guardian angel of my psyche
kept me pinned to the mattress, mindless and rapt.

Wearing Pencils

Here I am, ready to work:
lined, yellow-paper pad; pencil sharpened, in hand.
It's comical—

for now the waiting begins.
And with this, with the passing thought
my preparedness is comical,

it is Sunday morning again,
our family's dress-parade before the congregation
on route to our regular pew,

and I, garbed in a suit jacket, a miniature
of my father,
am drawing amused smiles from the adults we pass

for the five tall and sharp,
yellow pencils
lined up and on display in my breast-pocket.

There I was, ready to work.
I had brought no pad or paper.
If God wanted me to write, I suppose

I figured God would provide.
Maybe I was the paper.
Who knew?

I was prepared.
Now all I had to do was sit still
and wait.

Sin and Misery

We'd been best friends since the first day of first grade.
I stopped crying the moment I caught sight
of our female teacher, and relaxed,
and got on with the work of making my way
in a world populated solely with people
the same age and size as me,
and the two of us found each other.

How strange it was
to be collected together in a room
and made to sit in a chair
that was not a chair,
behind a table
that was not a table
but a kind of contraption without wheels,
and parked in rows, side by side,
like cars lined and waiting for the ferry.
Except there was no ferry,
and we weren't going anywhere.

Why were we being punished?
What had we done?

The next moment it is five years later,
and I have my former best friend
pinned to the ground.
His glasses may be broken.
I will be needing glasses myself soon.
He looks me in the eye and says,
in pain, with a slight smile, *You like this, don't you?*

Where did he get that line?
He means, *You like pinning me to the ground*
while our classmates stand around and laugh.
And I have to admit, though not aloud,
and not to him, that yes, I do,
I enjoy the power and license,
and would it be okay if I punched him in the face
for saying so? Instead,

I slowly rise, unpinning him, and walk away,
and that world blurs and fades.

My Dog Sandy

That autumn my father, offhandedly,
because he had no skill in this,
mentioned over the dinner table
that the family dog,
which we had left behind on a farm
when we moved halfway across the country,
had been shot, shot
in the head, my father said,
as a chicken killer.

I was not surprised the dog killed chickens,
but shot in the head
shut my throat.
I decided to think my father was cruel.

He, the dog, hadn't looked back
from the bed of the pickup truck of his new owner
when he drove off,
but this didn't surprise me, either.
And he wasn't the family dog, officially,
but mine,
the prize of much begging and many promises,
and a hope, I think, on my parents' part,
that it would help.

It takes a special kind of person
to turn a dog against you, but that's exactly
what I managed to do.
I knew that he didn't want to bare his teeth,
or bite, but I gave him no choice.

If something had gone terribly wrong
at home, or in my life, I'd like to know
what it was, and why, at eleven years of age,
I was so given to rage. Striking Sandy
was my way of saying, *Savage me,*
tear me apart—

                    a command he only obeyed
a few months later
on those poor chickens.

Good dog.

Dominion Day

In the schoolyard, that first day of summer,
Craig and I filled a bucket at the school's outdoor tap
and poured it down a gopher hole. Fill, pour, repeat.
Walking with the water sloshing between us
was laborious and slow, and I was convinced
our flash flood would soak into the earth
before we could top it up,
but two trips later success greeted us
in the form of a half-drowned creature
who struggled into daylight without
enough strength left in him to make
the slightest motion of protest when,
awed by consequence, we placed him
in the cardboard box one of us ran home to fetch.

The morning had begun with a BB gun,
and the two of us lying on our stomachs
in the dry grass, waiting for the gopher to emerge,
nose first, alert and ever-sniffing,
a model of animal caution as inch by inch
he rose to full height, and Craig fired.

The shot sent our quarry back down the hole,
and it was the morning gone, waiting
for him to reappear, that drove us
to search for a bucket, and the smudge
of blood on cardboard that told us why
he held his breath to almost the last gasp.

I raced my bike to Craig's the next day
to visit our wild pet, but the box was empty.
Thinking that our remorse and nursing care
would mend everything, my friend had picked up
the gopher, and was so surprised when the thing
bit him that he flung it into the road,
where that small animal of our childhood

hit the pavement running, he said,
and got the hell out of there.

Crack Shot

When he was eight years old, his father
gave him a BB gun for Christmas,
and taught him to shoot
by placing a tin can on a fence.
Once he could hit the can dead-on every time,
his father instructed him to shoot
while slowly sweeping the barrel left to right.
And when he could hit the target
dead-on every time, sweep right to left,
then ground to sky, then sky to ground.
When he never missed a shot,
his father flung a metal paint can lid into the air:
a gallon lid, a quart lid, a pint: the targets
got smaller and smaller
the sharper the boy's aim grew.

"How small did they get?" I ask, from the edge of my seat.
At this, James pulls from his pocket an envelope,
inside of which is the letter his father wrote
to his own father. It reads, *Dear Dad,*
see what a crack shot your grandson has become.
Inside the letter is a coin, a quarter,
which James now hands to me:
the heavily pock-marked souvenir
of when he reached the impossible heights of boyhood,
and could do anything that his eye desired.

His sights these days are focused on our daughter.
She and he arrived this Christmas morning
with news of their engagement.

They appeared at the door, both
stunned and happy. Before we sat to feast,
he took me aside to relate this story,
not by way of asking permission for her hand,
for we're long past that world, and not to say
that his aim is true, for we know this already.
I think he wants to tell us, in no
uncertain terms, and from the impossible
new heights they now share,
just how true that aim is.

The Beautiful Burn

In the church where we go to now
two people stand face to face
    on a Saturday afternoon, mid-spring.
They ask each other, Will you? Do you?
Shall we?
     Thus begins the dance.

The church where we go to now is a dance hall of heart and mind.
(Our bodies await further instruction.)
What we do here, the preacher says, is dance,
    fall down; dance, fall down....
Romance is a seven-letter word: one letter
    for each of the seven holy consecrated days of the week.
Each day with its saddlebag of pleasure and patch-kit.

The two new dance partners take hand in hand,
    and turn to face the witness of family, friend.
Thus begins the journey.
Outside, two bicycles lean one against the other.

How many revolutions has it been?
How many turns of the wheel since the one jogging beside you
    let go the saddle,
and you travelled a straight line to the curb,
and felt the sudden concrete against your skin
    burn
        the beautiful burn?

The one true revolution is love.

And if I do something truly unwise,
if, breezing down a hill, I try, at the bottom
            a ninety-degree turn, fail, go flying
                        into the curb, off the cliff,
and become a tangled catastrophe of flesh and blood,
make a mess, forget the milk, bring down the empire....

Love alters geography, softens concrete.

How many revolutions has it been, will it be?
The wheel turns, the world changes.
That little plastic gadget, attached to the handlebar,
            the one with the numbers on it,
will it also keep track of other distances,
the rise and fall in the heart rate we feel for each other?

The one true revolution is love.
Love makes a bike path through the wilderness
            of every holy, consecrated day.
It creates geography.

uphill
I'm half-crazy, all for the love
downhill
of long distance, riding-in-the-slipstream,
sore-ass
            touring
in tandem.
            Shall we?

Two lovers rise and stand in the midst of the people
on a Saturday afternoon, mid-spring.
They enter the witness of family, friend,
moving in sync.

FOR HEATHER AND JASON

Grasshopping

I knew I should have fixed the second-storey sunroom window sills
before the painters came,

and now that they're done and gone and the house
looks brand-spanking, it's depressing to think

the problem hasn't gone with them,
and that I'll be defacing the loveliness they brushed on

as soon as, one, I decide
how crazy-thorough a repair job to do,

and two, get around to doing it.
Note that this is precisely the type of upkeep issue

I'd strongly advise you not put off addressing
on your own home, should you call for consultation or a quote.

But there's maintenance, and there's maintenance.
Chez moi, I have things to do

that do not include
gathering tools or climbing a ladder,

unless that ladder be this sentence,
the short black legs of its 12-point typeface

trooping up the rungs like a line of ants—carpenter ants, let's say,
who have evolved, reformed

to be on our side now, and who,
for the fine work they are doing fixing those rotting sills,

ask as their only recompense
the poem I am composing down here in this lawn chair.

New Year, Good Work

The tools of the trade lay scattered on the floor
below the altar, migrating to its surface
(protected under plywood and a cloth tarp),
only after the first few days, when the fine mist
of wood dust that settled over the pews and furnishings
helped us to feel more at ease in this space
now sanctified to our labour.
Church interior as worksite.
I can think of worse ways to begin the year.

Moving through the motions of ritual
attendance to table saw, mitre saw,
in mindful repetition, alert, thinking
only of the blade, the cut, its closeness
to the mark, each length and angle made
to match another, to join in such perfection
as can be achieved on this job, in this lifetime.
And it's always fresh cut to fresh cut,
and there's something to that, but I can't think what.

A question formed itself as we chewed cuds
at break time, prompted by the vaulted ceiling
and the heartfelt, volunteer labour
of the two who started this project, who made
not a complete botch, but thank God
had no chainsaw handy to trim the wainscot.
The question? Ah, yes: our patron in this place,
was he a finish carpenter, or rough?

A lot of fancy woodwork's been performed
on his behalf. The romantic version has him
leaned over a plank, his two hands gripped
on a bench plane, a long shaving furled
round his wrist: the scroll that we apprentice-priests
of woodcraft must uncurl, to read the grain
wherein lies hid the meaning of life and death
and pretty much everything in between.

Did he enjoy the fine work, or prefer
to hammer studs; to kiss that sixteenth of an inch,
or was close enough, good enough?
What were his tolerances, professionally?
Could he make it less than perfect? Did he measure
once? And how did he balance the desire to do it well
with the need to get it done?

These and other questions will be answered
Sunday morning by his current rep,
who'll stand behind the pulpit we've restored,
and packed our tools, and collected and swept
the scraps and shavings, and vacuumed up the dust—
though later we will hear how the incense of our craft
and labour lingered in the sanctuary air that day,
as answered prayer for good work, done—
which is all we need to know, and answer enough.

Faith of Our Fathers

When I was young and sitting in church
we used to sing, *Faith of Our Fathers*,
a rouser of a hymn, in which we braved
dungeon, fire and sword, and stayed true till death.

What was our father up to
while my sisters and brother and I slept
or sat in school,
and did mom know, and what was faith
that he was getting us into so much trouble for?

At the same time you could tell
it wasn't our own flesh-and-blood dad
sitting next to us in the pew that the song was about,
though he sang loud and strong
like it was great we could all be in jail together,

so maybe it was his father,
the older, kind-looking man in the photograph,
whom we children of immigrants wanted to
but never met—which seemed even less likely.

The song said their faith was *living still*,
meaning it hadn't died; father after father,
all down the line, they'd passed it on,
kept it going, like a small fire,

a life-giving flame that cooked their food
and warmed their bones, and that when push
came to shove they'd fight to hang onto,
though this hadn't happened in a long time.

Or maybe *living still* meant their faith was quiet and calm,
reflective, like flood waters in the lowlands
on a windless day. Or both.
But what was it? Faith?
I still didn't know. Something to do

with fire and water. Because he was my father,
and because mom did know, and agreed,
I have carried the fire and entered the water
also singing, although the words now are changed
and we brave not dungeon and sword
but doubt and difference, while staying true
to sweetness words could not touch,
but poured from their mouths like honey.

White Chapel

My parents lie buried together
between a highway and hydro towers
in a row,
and each time I visit,
which is not often, I admit,
I have trouble locating their flat plaque
in the acres of grass that roll like the ocean.

They are flotsam, I think.
They float, not sink, along with every other
briefcase-size plaque
that surrounds the ghost-ship white
steel-sided chapel
that rides the green-bladed swell
and indiscernible currents.

When I find them at last,
their heads on one pillow,
half the time is spent taking my bearings,
hoping to fix their place in my mind
for the next visit,
though it's never yet helped.

I look down to their bronze names,
then up to the few planted trees,
and note a memorial bench
a few degrees to the left
in this featureless landscape
dedicated to death and ease
of maintenance.

The larger than life, stone white
Jesus who's planted close to the exit
is down on his knees, arms outstretched
telling the dead how sorry he is
that it's come to this.
He feels nothing but grief
I can tell.

My good old dad was a practical man
for which I am mostly grateful.
We had only to add the date of his demise
to the waiting plaque,
and to stand beside the open hole,
then return to our cars.

He'd purchased a package deal
from a fellow immigrant,
and there are other names here that I recognize,
more folk of their generation
likewise flattened to the ground,
who answered the call of loyalty
and supporting their own
by writing a cheque: Dutch names
floating in an open sea of English
and Scot, Italian and German and Pole.

Fifteen years later we pulled back the covers
to lay mom beside him, and learned,
while signing papers in the White Chapel office,

that they, my parents, had room below
for company.

My wife, whom they loved, and who loved them,
has no qualms or misgivings
about bunking in:
One stop shopping for our kids, she says.
She takes after my father more than I,
who was truly creeped out,
at first, by the notion,
but am getting there, slowly,
laboriously, to the edge,
one step at a time, shuffling,
and may finally consent, and fall in.

She says, from the reclining chair
across our living room, *I don't really care.*
Meaning, it makes no difference to her
where she is laid to rest.
And neither do I
care, yet it seems that I do.

It is such a pleasure to walk through
the old graveyard close to our home,
among the chiselled blocks and obelisks,
with their names and dates and generations
of strangers, the extended civic family, who leave notes
on the kitchen table, *You are forever*
in our hearts, with little-lamb hints

of their miseries. The mystery
that death brings to life
is less unfriendly there, more lived-in,
inhabitable. At White Chapel
Memorial Gardens I feel nothing but grief
for a world that strips the earth
down to its bones.

We last visited the site
where our parents lie buried
when my sister and brother-in-law
were in town for Easter weekend:
four of us searching in the grass
yet again for that plaque.
Maybe it makes sense
for them to be buried and lost
in this green sea, floating
forever between the country they were born in
and the one they moved to.

We looked down at their bronze names,
and nestled a few, small chocolate eggs
between the letters, then took a photo
and sent it to our far-flung family
in real time, right
from where we were standing.
It felt like something. It tasted
a little like redemption

which I hope by now I've learned to accept
wherever I'm lucky enough to find it,
or it finds me.

The Back Way

At sixteen, when she had earned
her driver's licence and was allowed
to use the family station wagon
to go to the mall or her part-time job,
she always took the back way, she says.

She says this as we ramp up
to join US 46, merge
onto the Garden State Parkway, exit
to Route 4, to reach Route 17
with its classic, only-in-New Jersey
six lanes of traffic
off which are driveways.

Fifteen minutes of sheer terror
and we are sitting at a table
in the Suburban Diner
waiting to have dinner
with family friends from her old neighbourhood.

The back way explains why
she is not familiar with the highways
she grew up among, whereas the winding
two-way streets and roads
she always chose instead
still feel as natural as water,

yet after forty years
of only intermittent visits

the compass by which she followed
those paths of least resistance
is not so reliable, and we are lost
more than once.

We will be un-lost, I'm sure
if we stay a few days more.
The needle will point true,
landmarks fall back into place.
But why stay? There's no one here
to call or hold us.

Today we joined her family in the park;
past the reflecting pool,
third tree on the left, six rows in,
where grass over-growing the two plaques
(one for her parents, one for three brothers)
doesn't quite hide
the names that young Joe groundskeeper,
with shovel and dust broom,
helps us to uncover.

It's been ten years since our last visit,
twenty since the passing
of the family's next-to-last survivor,
her mother. We are far from home,
our home, though this is still home too.
Mine as well as hers. And the back way
is how we got here,

with no guide or global positioning system
to ease the confusion,
the travelling in circles, questions

and no need to fill the dead silence in the car
that seems eternal
but is simply two people
riding out their aloneness
on the return trip,
communing, if they can,
with every one who has left them so far behind.

Egg Plant

You're too young, the Italian matron wailed
in mock despair, and with much gesturing,
when she learned that at the tender age of twenty-one
I was already married.

Or real despair. It was hard to tell. I should be
like her son, she cried, who was out
having a good time now
but would settle down soon enough.
What was I thinking?

We had come to paint her porch, my boss and I.
He was not much older than me,
and also married. There was a lot of that
going around then, among our kind.

I shrugged my shoulders and grinned
the crazy, lopsided grin that always won the girl.
What could I say? *Stupido mio!*
I had no such grin, by the way.

Standing in the early morning sun
being reamed out, playfully or in earnest,
the captive audience
of a very expressive Italian *donna,*

reminded me of my previous job
in an egg grading plant,
earning the money to get married,
in the company of seven, black-clad Italian women

who arrived to work each morning
squeezed into one taxi.

I was not squeezed into the taxi with them
but came by bus, alone,
walking in darkness to my stop
with only the morning star in the sky to give me hope
that these days would not last forever.

In the plant, the women rotated every hour
through the various stations of the monster contraption,
one to feed its insatiable hunger
with trays of eggs by the cartful,
two to candle in a booth for blood spots,
and four to pluck the bobbing ovals
from the conveyor belt
and place them into cartons.

My task was to supply the carts
and carry the boxed cartons back to the cooler.
It was as mindless and boring
as the life of a chicken, and I fought to stay sane
while aching with absence for the loved one.

The only relief came on some long afternoons
when over the clacking of the machinery
one of the women began to sing
a slow and mournful tune, in her native tongue,
which her compatriots would join,
their voices rising to the fans and fluorescent lights,

a song that caught and held the moment
in an egg grading plant, in an industrial park
beside a highway, and made it heaven.

And so I fell in love
with the redemptive power of art,
or its sweet delusion,
and with seven Italian *signore*
whom I nevertheless left forever two months later
to marry an Anglo-Dutch chick
more my own age
and live happily ever after,

but if one of their kind
now wanted to ream me out,
playfully or in earnest, from her front porch
in broad daylight, for choosing to take flight
with a bird of like feather
rather than free range,
I would accept this criticism
with a grin which never won me any girl
save one.

Acknowledgements & Notes

"Poetry Burns" is a found poem, lifted whole from the pages of the *Hamilton Spectator* (February 9, 2001). "North of Sixty" appeared in *Fiddlehead* no.265 (Autumn 2015). "Night Bus" is for Michael Vander Weele. "Neighbour" and "Needlecraft" were previously published in the chapbook *Brendan Luck* (Gaspereau Press, 2005). "Needlecraft" also appeared in *Reformed Worship*, and won an Evangelical Press of America Prize for Poetry (2009). "A Common Thread" was written for the opening of a posthumous show for Robert Vander Plaats; a selection of one hundred of the more than thousand mandala paintings he created because this was the only thing, he said, that kept the voices at bay. Thank you to Peter Reitsma, for asking. The poem was published in the special Alice Munro issue of *Windsor Review* vol.47, no.2 (Fall 2014). The first half also found its way into *Christian Courier*. Thanks to Tim (JR) Struthers for his immaculate editorial eye. "Near-Annunciation at Carroll's Point" and "New Year, Good Work" appeared in *Image* 87 (Winter 2015), and also in *The Turning Aside: The Kingdom Poets Book of Contemporary Christian Poetry*, D.S. Martin, ed. (Wipf & Stock, 2016). "Plight" was written for, and read at, the *Welcome to Hamilton* concert to benefit youth programs for recent Syrian refugees, May 13, 2016. "Orange and Spices" was written for *Image Journal* in response to their request for a poem on a theme of science and faith. It appeared in *Image* 85 (Summer 2015). The genesis of the poem is a story Ron Gabor told me from his days working at McMaster University's Mills Memorial Library in Hamilton. "The Tin Box", "After Catechism Class", "Wearing Pencils", "Sin and Misery" and "Dominion Day" appeared in *Antigonish Review* no.181 (Spring 2015). The closing line of "Catechism Class" is a nod to Micah Lexier's 1980 art installation at the Hamilton Central Library, *I wouldn't be surprised if that's not the whole story*. He found this line quoted in a story from the *Hamilton Spectator*. "Vocation" appeared in *Grain* vol.42, no.4 (Summer 2015), and was selected for *Best Canadian Poetry* 2016, Helen Humphreys, ed. (Tightrope Books, 2016). "Wearing Pencils", "New Year, Good Work", "Night Bus" and "Catechism Class" each appeared in separate issues of the annual student literary publication, *Openings*, at my almost-alma-mater, Trinity Christian College, in the southwest Chicago town of Palos Heights. "The Beautiful Burn" was written for Heather and Jason, because they asked, and read at their wedding, to the piano accompaniment of Bart Nameth. It appeared in *Hammered Out*. "Grasshopping" appeared in *A Chevron of Geese*, a fund-raising chapbook published by gritLIT, Hamilton's literary festival (2014). "Faith of Our Fathers" appeared in *The Banner* (June 2017).

The body type, CALIFORNIAN, was originally designed as a proprietary typeface for the University of California Press in 1938 by the American type designer Frederic Goudy. Released to the general trade by Lanston Monotype in 1956, it is infrequently seen in use these days; Goudy's idiosyncratic romans and italics seem to have lost their currency, and making the digital revivals of his typefaces sparkle on the smooth sheets and screens of the post-letterpress age takes an experienced hand. Still, these letters embody a quirky warmth and humanity worth preserving.

The display type, VAN LANEN, is a wedge-serifed homage to the wooden display types of the nineteenth century designed by Matthew Carter. It was both issued in digital form by P22 Type Foundry and cut in wood at the Hamilton Wood Type & Printing Museum in Two Rivers, Wisconsin, in 2002.

¶ This project was funded, in part, by the Government of Canada (Financé par le gouvernement du Canada) through the Canada Council for the Arts and the Canada Book Fund, and in partnership with the Province of Nova Scotia. ¶ This book was edited and designed by Andrew Steeves and printed offset and bound under the direction of Gary Dunfield at Gaspereau Press.

7 6 5 4 3 2 1

Library & Archives Canada Cataloguing in Publication

Terpstra, John, author
Mischief / John Terpstra.

Poems.
ISBN 978-1-55447-167-6 (softcover)
I. Title.

PS8589.E75M57 2017 C811'.54 C2017-900352-6

GASPEREAU PRESS LIMITED ¶ GARY DUNFIELD & ANDREW STEEVES ¶ PRINTERS & PUBLISHERS
47 Church Avenue, Kentville, Nova Scotia B4N 2M7
Literary Outfitters & Cultural Wilderness Guides